★★
★ *The Library of*
American Landmarks™

THE STATUE OF LIBERTY

Gina Strazzabosco-Hayn

The Rosen Publishing Group's

PowerKids Press™
New York

Published in 1997 by The Rosen Publishing Group, Inc.
29 East 21st Street, New York, NY 10010

First Edition

Book Design: Danielle Primiceri

Photo Credits: Cover © Orion/International Stock; p. 4 © Dennis Hallinan/FPG International Corp.; p. 7 (large photo and inset) © AP/Wide World Photos; pp. 8, 15, 19 © Photoworld/FPG International Corp.; p. 11 © Fergus O'Brien/FPG International Corp.; p. 12 © FPG International Corp.; p. 16 © C. Reaves/FPG International Corp.; p. 20 © Pcholkin, Vladimir/FPG International Corp.

Strazzabosco-Hayn, Gina.
    The Statue of Liberty / by Gina Strazzabosco-Hayn.
        p.   cm. — (The library of American Landmarks)
    Includes index.
    Summary: Describes the planning and building of the Statue of Liberty by the French as a gift to the United States.
    ISBN 0-8239-5018-2
    1. Statue of Liberty (New York, NY)—History—Juvenile literature. 2. New York (NY)—Buildings, structures, etc.—Juvenile literature. [1. Statue of Liberty (New York, NY) 2. National monuments. 3. Statues.] I. Title. II. Series.
F128.64.L6S76 1997
974.7'1—dc21
                                    97-14513
                                    CIP
                                    AC

Manufactured in the United States of America

Table of Contents

In Honor of Liberty

As a result of the Revolutionary War, the thirteen **colonies** (KOL-uh-neez) won their freedom from British rule and became the United States of America. This new country promised its people **democracy** (de-MOK-ruh-see) and **liberty** (LIB-er-tee).

In 1865, Frenchman Édouard de Laboulaye wanted to give the United States a great statue in honor of its **independence** (in-dee-PEN-dents) and liberty. He hoped that the French would use these ideas in their own country as well.

◄ The Statue of Liberty has come to stand for the opportunities available in the United States.

Friendship Between Countries

Laboulaye shared his idea with a young artist, Frédéric Auguste Bartholdi. Bartholdi was famous for creating large **sculptures** (SKULP-cherz).

Bartholdi believed in the same things that Laboulaye did. He loved the idea of creating a **monument** (MON-yoo-ment) that stood for those beliefs. He and Laboulaye thought that giving a great monument to the United States would help build a friendship between the two countries.

Frédéric Bartholdi (lower photo) helped shape Édouard de Laboulaye's ideas into a giant statue. ▶

NEW YORK

CONNECTICUT

PENNSYLVANIA

THE STATUE OF LIBERTY

NEW JERSEY

A Visit to the United States

In 1871, Bartholdi visited the United States to present the idea of a statue to the American people. As Bartholdi's ship pulled into New York Harbor, he saw tiny Bedloe Island. He decided that it would be the perfect place for his statue.

Bartholdi soon drew a sketch of the image he would build: A woman wearing a robe and holding a torch that stood for liberty. He first called the statue Liberty Enlightening the World. It was later shortened to the Statue of Liberty.

◀ The Statue of Liberty is sometimes called Lady Liberty.

The First Step

In the United States, Bartholdi met with the president, governors, senators, writers, and many other important people to tell them about the statue. Many people liked the idea of the statue, but some didn't.

Because it was going to be a very **expensive** (ek-SPEN-siv) project, many people agreed that France would have to take the first step. So Bartholdi returned to France to start raising money for his giant statue.

Bartholdi was determined to build his statue, no matter how much money it would cost. ▶

Raising Money

Laboulaye and Bartholdi hoped to have the statue finished by 1876, which was the 100th birthday of the United States. But they had a hard time raising money to pay for it.

In 1874, France and the United States decided to share the cost. France would pay for the statue, and the United States would pay for the **pedestal** (PED-es-tul) on which it would stand. Finally, the French raised enough money for Bartholdi to begin building the statue at his studio in Paris.

Despite the size of the giant statue, Bartholdi created lots of detail such as the knuckles in her hand.

One Piece Finished

By 1876, Bartholdi had finished the arm holding the torch. This was sent to the United States to help raise American interest and money for the pedestal. People could pay 50 cents to climb the stairs to the torch.

Many newspapers and magazines printed articles about Bartholdi and his project. But few Americans **donated** (DOH-nay-ted) money for the pedestal. That didn't matter to Bartholdi. He continued to work on the statue.

Today, the arm and torch are no longer open to the public. ▶

Reaching the Goal

Bartholdi finished the statue in 1884. It was presented to the United States, but was held in Paris because there still was not enough money to build the pedestal. Joseph Pulitzer, publisher of *The World*, a New York newspaper, decided to help. He offered to print in his newspaper the name of each person who gave money for the statue.

Thousands of men, women, and children sent in what they could—pennies, dollars, even two chickens. By August 1885, 120,000 people had donated $102,000. Finally, the pedestal could be built.

◀ The base of the statue is an eleven-pointed star that was part of a fort.

Finally in Place

While the pedestal was being built, the French shipped the completed statue to the United States.

The pedestal was finished in April 1886. An engineer named Gustave Eiffel designed the iron frame that went inside the statue. He built the frame to withstand the strong winds that blew across the bay where the statue would stand. Then the bronze plates of the statue itself were attached to the frame. Six months later, the Statue of Liberty was finally standing in place.

Today, you can climb all the way up to the top of the statue and look out of the windows in her crown. ▶

Liberty Stands Tall

At 305 feet, the statue was the tallest **structure** (STRUK-sher) in New York City at that time. In one arm, she holds a tablet that says "July 4, 1776," the date the Declaration of Independence was signed.

On the pedestal is a **plaque** (PLAK) with a poem on it. This poem was written in 1883 by a woman named Emma Lazarus. Her words speak to all people coming to the United States in search of a better life.

It took a long time to get the Statue of Liberty in place. But on October 28, 1886, thousands of people celebrated her arrival.

◀ The Statue of Liberty is often the center of America's celebrations such as the Fourth of July.

Freedom and Hope

The Statue of Liberty has become a **symbol** (SIM-bul) of freedom around the world. She was the first thing that many **immigrants** (IM-ih-grents) saw when they came to the United States. To them, the statue symbolized the hope of a better future.

During the 1920s, President Calvin Coolidge named the statue a national monument. Today, the National Park Service takes care of the statue and Liberty Island. They help to make sure that the Statue of Liberty will stand for many years to come.

Glossary

colony (KOL-uh-nee) An area in a new country where a large group of people move but who remain under the rule of their own country.

democracy (de-MOK-ruh-see) A government that is run by the people.

donate (DOH-nayt) To give a gift of money or help.

expensive (ek-SPEN-siv) To cost a lot of money.

immigrant (IM-ih-grent) A person who moves to another country to live.

independence (in-dee-PEN-dents) When a country rules itself.

liberty (LIB-er-tee) The freedom or the right to do as one wants.

monument (MON-yoo-ment) A statue, plaque, or building that honors a person, idea, or event.

pedestal (PED-es-tul) A base on which a statue stands.

plaque (PLAK) A thin piece of metal with words written on it.

sculpture (SKULP-cher) A figure that is carved or formed.

structure (STRUK-sher) Something that is built, such as a building or a statue.

symbol (SIM-bul) Something that stands for something else.

Index